I0706802

Malala Yousafzai:
A Voice for the Voiceless

Malala Yousafzai was born on July 12, 1997, into a family that cherished education and held progressive ideals close to their hearts. Hailing from the picturesque yet turbulent Swat Valley in Pakistan, Malala was brought up in an environment that nurtured her sense of justice and instilled in her a deep-rooted passion for learning, a passion that would shape her destiny in profound ways.

Malala's family background and cultural influences were pivotal in shaping her character and activism. Her father, Ziauddin Yousafzai, a renowned educational activist and poet, was a driving force behind Malala's unwavering pursuit of education and equality. Ziauddin's unshakable belief in the power of education, despite the oppressive social norms prevailing in Swat Valley, inspired Malala from an early age. Her mother, Toor Pekai, a strong and resilient woman, also played a pivotal role in nurturing Malala's spirit, imbuing in her a sense of purpose and determination to challenge societal norms.

As a child growing up in Mingora, Swat Valley, Malala's world was a vibrant tapestry of breathtaking landscapes and rich cultural heritage.

She reveled in the beauty of Swat Valley, with its lush green valleys, towering mountains, and flowing rivers, which stirred her love for nature and deep sense of belonging to her homeland. However, Swat Valley was not immune to the dark clouds of extremism and oppression, which would soon cast their shadows over Malala's idyllic childhood.

Despite the challenges posed by a regressive society, Malala's early passion for education burned brightly. She was an avid reader, voraciously consuming books and devouring knowledge with an insatiable thirst for learning. Her fervor for education was matched by her unwavering determination to fight against the injustices faced by girls in her community, who were often deprived of their right to education. Malala's interest in activism was ignited by her father's influence and her own firsthand experiences of witnessing the denial of education to girls in Swat Valley.

At a tender age, Malala began writing a blog for BBC Urdu under a pseudonym, eloquently documenting her experiences and advocating for girls' education. Her writings were a clarion call for equality, an unwavering voice against the oppressive forces that sought to silence her. Her fearless activism, coupled with her undeniable eloquence and conviction, captured the attention of the world and earned her widespread acclaim as a symbol of hope and resilience in the face of adversity.

Taliban Attack and Global Outrage

The rise of the Taliban in Swat Valley, Pakistan, in the early 2000s cast a dark shadow over Malala Yousafzai's valiant efforts to promote education and empower girls. The Taliban's oppressive rule, with their brutal interpretation of Islamic law, resulted in the closure of schools and the denial of basic rights to women, plunging the region into darkness.

Despite the growing threat, Malala remained unwavering in her mission to advocate for education. Her defiance against the Taliban's extremist ideology was a beacon of hope in the face of adversity. However, her courage and determination made her a target.

On October 9, 2012, the world was stunned by a heinous act of violence that shook the global conscience. Malala, then just 15 years old, and her classmates were ambushed by the Taliban on their school bus. Malala was shot in the head, the bullet narrowly missing her brain, but leaving her gravely injured. The attack was a cowardly attempt to silence a young girl who dared to speak out against oppression, but it only served to amplify her voice.

The global outrage that followed the attack was swift and resolute. Leaders, activists, and ordinary people from all walks of life condemned the senseless violence and expressed their solidarity with Malala.

Her story struck a chord with millions who saw her as a symbol of courage and hope in the face of brutality.

The attack on Malala brought to light the plight of girls' education and women's rights in Pakistan and beyond. The Taliban's restrictive policies and their brutal methods of enforcing their extremist ideology were exposed to the world. Malala's determination to promote education and gender equality resonated with people of all backgrounds, cultures, and religions.

The hashtag #IamMalala trended on social media, with people from around the world sharing messages of support and solidarity. Petitions were signed, rallies were held, and Malala's story became a rallying cry for change. Her courage and resilience in the face of adversity inspired millions, igniting a global movement to support her cause.

Recovery and Resilience

Malala Yousafzai's road to recovery after the heinous attack by the Taliban was nothing short of remarkable. Her indomitable spirit and unwavering determination to continue her activism for girls' education and human rights served as an inspiration to the world, showcasing her resilience in the face of adversity.

Following the attack, Malala was swiftly airlifted to the United Kingdom for specialized medical treatment. The bullet that had pierced her head was removed, and she underwent a series of surgeries and rehabilitation to address her injuries. The global community rallied around her, offering support, prayers, and well-wishes for her speedy recovery.

Malala's voice grew even louder during her recovery as she took her advocacy efforts to the global stage. She fearlessly spoke out about the importance of education and gender equality in numerous international forums. Her impassioned speeches captivated audiences and further amplified her message, earning her widespread acclaim for her courage and resilience.

In addition to her advocacy for girls' education, Malala also became a prominent voice for human rights, particularly the rights of children and women. She used her platform to highlight the injustices faced by marginalized communities and to call for equality, justice, and peace. Her commitment to her cause and her resilience in the face of adversity made her a global symbol of hope and inspiration.

Malala's activism transcended borders and cultures, resonating with people from all walks of life. Her message of empowerment through education, her courage in the face of oppression, and her resilience captured the hearts and minds of millions around the world.

She became a symbol of hope for those who faced similar challenges and a beacon of inspiration for those who sought to make a difference in their communities.

Education and Activism

Malala Yousafzai's commitment to education and girls' rights continued to shine brightly as she embarked on a global journey to promote her cause and create positive change. Her activism extended far beyond her home country of Pakistan, as she fearlessly spoke out on international stages, founded the Malala Fund, and made a lasting impact on girls' education worldwide.

After recovering from the attack by the Taliban, Malala became an even more vocal advocate for education and girls' rights on a global scale. Her speeches at the United Nations and other international forums were powerful and poignant, capturing the attention and hearts of audiences worldwide. Her eloquence, poise, and determination to promote education for all children, regardless of gender or background, made her a formidable force in the global movement for education and human rights.

Building on her advocacy efforts, Malala co-founded the Malala Fund, a nonprofit organization focused on advocating for girls' education and empowering young girls to achieve their potential through education.

The Malala Fund works to remove barriers to education, including poverty, discrimination, and violence, and promotes girls' right to 12 years of free, quality education.

The impact of the Malala Fund has been far-reaching. The organization has funded education programs in countries such as Pakistan, Nigeria, Jordan, and Lebanon, providing access to education for thousands of girls who face systemic barriers to education. The Malala Fund has also partnered with global leaders, organizations, and philanthropists to amplify its mission and create lasting change.

Personal and Professional Growth

After the traumatic attack by the Taliban, Malala's road to recovery included not only physical healing but also a strong commitment to her education. She continued her studies and pursued further education in the United Kingdom, where she and her family eventually settled after seeking medical treatment.

As Malala's global profile rose, she also found her voice as a writer. In 2013, she published her memoir, "I Am Malala: The Girl Who Stood Up for Education and Was Shot by the Taliban." The memoir, co-written with British journalist Christina Lamb, detailed Malala's journey, her passion for education, and her fight for girls' rights.

The book became an international bestseller, capturing the hearts and minds of readers worldwide, and further amplifying Malala's message and impact.

In addition to her memoir, Malala has continued to use her writing skills to advocate for education and social change. She has penned numerous op-eds and articles for major publications, where she has eloquently articulated her vision for a more just and equitable world. Her powerful words have served as a rallying cry for the importance of education, gender equality, and human rights, inspiring millions to join her cause and take action.

Recognitions and Awards

In 2014, Malala's tireless efforts and remarkable achievements were honored with the Nobel Peace Prize, making her the youngest-ever recipient of this prestigious award. At the age of 17, Malala stood on the global stage in Oslo, Norway, to accept the award, delivering a powerful acceptance speech that called for worldwide access to education and an end to discrimination against girls. Her eloquence and poise captivated audiences, and her determination to continue her activism despite facing grave dangers was truly awe-inspiring.

In addition to the Nobel Peace Prize, Malala has received numerous other awards and honors for her advocacy and activism. She has been awarded honorary Canadian citizenship, become a United Nations Messenger of Peace, and been recognized by organizations such as Amnesty International, the Harvard Foundation, and the United Nations Foundation for her outstanding contributions to human rights and global education initiatives.

Malala Yousafzai's journey from a young girl advocating for girls' education in Pakistan to a global icon of social change and empowerment has been nothing short of extraordinary. Her resilience, courage, and commitment to her cause have inspired millions around the world. Through her advocacy, philanthropic efforts, and various projects, Malala has made a lasting impact on girls' education and human rights, while also paving the way for future generations of activists.

Her speeches and interviews are filled with powerful and insightful words that highlight the importance of education, equality, and social justice. They encapsulate her unwavering advocacy for the rights of girls and the power of education to transform lives. Her words inspire others to stand up, speak out, and make a positive difference in the world. In this collection of quotations, you will find Malala's empowering words that continue to inspire and resonate with people of all ages and backgrounds.

Let us wage a glorious
struggle against
illiteracy, poverty
and terrorism, let us
pick up our books and
our pens, they are the
most powerful weapons.
One child, one teacher,
one book and one pen
can change the world.
Education is the only
solution.

I have the right of
education. I have the
right to play. I have
the right to sing.
I have the right to
talk. I have the right
to go to market.
I have the right
to speak up.

In his pocket he [Malala's father] kept a poem written by Martin Niemöller, who had lived in Nazi Germany.

First they came for the communists, and I didn't speak out because I wasn't a communist. Then they came for the socialists, and I didn't speak out because I wasn't a socialist. Then they came for the trade unionists, and I didn't speak out because I wasn't a trade unionist. Then they came for the Jews, and I didn't speak out because I was not a Jew. Then they came for the Catholics, and I didn't speak out because I was not a Catholic. Then they came for me, and there was no one left to speak for me.

We call upon all
communities to be
tolerant, to reject
prejudice based on
caste, creed, sect,
colour, religion or
agenda to ensure
freedom and equality
for women so they can
flourish. We cannot
all succeed when half
of us are held back.

We Pashtuns love
shoes but don't love
the cobbler; we love
our scarves and
blankets but do not
respect the weaver.
Manual workers made
a great contribution
to our society but
received no
recognition, and
this is the reason so
many of them joined
the Taliban—to
finally achieve
status and power.

Our men think earning
money and ordering
around others is
where power lies.
They don't think power
is in the hands of the
woman who takes care
of everyone all day
long, and gives birth
to their children.

Instead of sending
guns, send books.
Instead of sending
weapons, send
teachers.

Freedom is not worth
having if it does not
include the freedom
to make mistakes.

A city without books,
a city without a
library is like a
graveyard.

I said to myself,
Malala, you must be
brave. You must not be
afraid of anyone.
You are only trying
to get an education.
You are not
committing
a crime.

Weakness, fear and
hopelessness died.
Strength, power and
courage was born.

Outside his office my father had a framed copy of a letter written by Abraham Lincoln to his son's teacher, translated into Pashto. It is a very beautiful letter, full of good advice. Teach him, if you can, the wonder of books...But also give him quiet time to ponder the eternal mystery of birds in the sky, bees in the sun, and the flowers on a green hillside, it says. Teach him it is far more honorable to fail than to cheat.

Every girl deserves
to take part in
creating the
technology that will
change our world and
change who runs it.

So today, we call upon
the world leaders to
change their strategic
policies in favor of
peace and prosperity.
We call upon the world
leaders that all of
these deals must
protect women and
children's rights.
A deal that goes
against the rights of
women is unacceptable.

We will continue our
journey to our destination
of peace and education.
No one can stop us. We will
speak up for our rights and
we will bring change to our
voice. We believe in the
power and the strength of
our words. Our words can
change the whole world
because we are all together,
united for the cause of
education. And if we want to
achieve our goal, then let us
empower ourselves with the
weapon of knowledge and let
us shield ourselves with
unity and togetherness.

I learned another lesson watching the show [Ugly Betty]. Although Betty and her friends had certain rights, women in the United States were still not completely equal; their images were used to sell things. In some ways, I decided, women are showpieces in American society, too.

I was reminded of our history lessons, in which we learned about the loot or bounty an army enjoys when a battle is won. I began to see the awards and recognition just like that. They were little jewels without much meaning. I needed to concentrate on winning the war.

When someone tells me
about Malala, the girl
who was shot by the
Taliban - that's my
definition for her - I
don't think she's me.
Now I don't even feel
as if I was shot. Even
my life in Swat feels
like a part of history
or a movie I watched.
Things change. God
has given us a brain
and a heart which tell
us how to live.

It does not matter
what's the colour of
your skin, what
language do you
speak, what religion
do you believe in.
It is that we should
all consider each
other as human beings
and we should respect
each other.

Don't kill doves in the garden. You kill one and the others won't come.

Does not matter what
language you choose,
the important thing
is the words you use
to express yourself.

I think.... living in
such a hard situation
when there are
terrorists and they
slaughter people every
night is still hard — is
still a threat. So it's a
better idea to speak out
for your rights and then
die... we will speak out
for our rights. This is
what we can do, and we
tried our best.

I tell my story, not
because it is unique,
but because it is not.
It is the story of
many girls.

My father says that in our part of the world this idea of jihad was very much encouraged by the CIA. Children in the refugee camps were even given school textbooks produced by an American university which taught basic arithmetic through fighting. They had examples like "If out of 10 Russian infidels, 5 are killed by one Muslim, 5 would be left" or "15 bullets - 10 bullets = 5 bullets."

Once I had asked God
for one or two extra
inches in height, but
instead he made me as
tall as the sky, so
high that I could not
measure myself.

Ignorance allowed
politicians to fool
people and bad
administrators
to be re-elected.

To sit down on a
chair and read my
books with all my
friends at school is
my right. To see each
and every human
being with a smile of
happiness is my wish.
I am Malala. My world
has changed but I
have not.

Some people only
ask others to do
something.
I believe that, why
should I wait for
someone else? Why
don't I take a step
and move forward.

Even if you win three
or four times, the
next victory will not
necessarily be yours
without trying.

I do not remember a thing about the shooting. Not a single thing. The doctors and nurses offered complicated explanations for why I didn't recall the attack. They said the brain protects us from memories that are too painful to remember. Or, they said, my brain might have shut down as soon as I was injured. I love science, and I love nothing more than asking question upon question to figure out the way things work. But I don't need science to figure out why I don't remember the attack. I know why: God is kind to me.

To me, the moral of
the story was that
there will always be
hurdles in life, but
if you want to
achieve a goal, you
must continue.

Is Islam such a weak
religion that it
cannot tolerate a
book written against
it? Not my Islam!

Some people are
afraid of ghosts, some
of spiders or snakes—
in those days we were
afraid of our fellow
human beings.

Education is
education. We should
learn everything and
then choose which
path to follow.
Education is neither
Eastern nor Western,
it is human.

The Taliban could
take our pens and
books, but they
couldn't stop our
minds from thinking.

If people were silent
nothing would
change.

"We don't have any option. We are dependent on these mullahs to learn the Quran," he said. "But you just use him to learn the literal meaning of the words; don't follow his explanations and interpretation. Only learn what God says. His words are divine messages, which you are free and independent to interpret."

I believe the gun has
no power because a
gun can only kill,
but a pen can give
life.

I do not even hate the Talib who shot me. Even if there was a gun in my hand and he was standing in front of me, I would not shoot him. This is the compassion I have learned from Mohammed, the prophet of mercy, Jesus Christ and Lord Buddha. This the legacy of change I have inherited from Martin Luther King, Nelson Mandela and Mohammed Ali Jinnah. This is the philosophy of nonviolence that I have learned from Gandhi, Bacha Khan and Mother Teresa. And this is the forgiveness that I have learned from my father and from my mother. This is what my soul is telling me: be peaceful and love everyone.

If you want to resolve
a dispute, or come out
from conflict, the
very first thing is to
speak the truth.
If you have a
headache, and tell
the doctor you have a
stomach ache, how can
the doctor help? You
must speak the truth.
The truth will
abolish fear.

We realize the
importance of our
voices only when we
are silenced.

A girl has the power
to go forward in her
life. And she's not
only a mother, she's
not only a sister,
she's not only a wife.
But a girl has the -
she should have an
identity. She should
be recognized and she
has equal rights as a
boy.

Our Butkara ruins were a magical place to play hide-and-seek. Once some foreign archaeologists arrived to do some work there and told us that in times gone by it was a place of pilgrimage, full of beautiful temples domed with gold where Buddhist kings lay buried. My father wrote a poem, "The Relics of Butkara," which summed up perfectly how temple and mosque could exist side by side:

When the voice of truth rises from the minarets, / The Buddha smiles, / And the broken chain of history reconnects.

We like to put sacred texts in flowing waters, so I rolled it up, tied it to a piece of wood, placed a dandelion on top, and floated it in the stream which flows into the Swat River. Surely God would find it there.

We human beings don't
realize how great God is.
He has given us an
extraordinary brain and
a sensitive loving heart.
He has blessed us with
two lips to talk and
express our feelings, two
eyes which see a world of
colors and beauty, two
feet which walk on the
road of life, two hands to
work for us, a nose which
smells the beauty of
fragrance, and two ears
to hear the words of love.

Kindness can only be
repaid with kindness.
It can't be repaid
with expressions
like 'thank you' and
then forgotten.

Peace in every home, every street, every village, every country - this is my dream. Education for every boy and every girl in the world. To sit down on a chair and read my books with all my friends at school is my right. To see each and every human being with a smile of happiness is my wish.

I was a girl in a land
where rifles are fired
in celebration of a
son, while daughters
are hidden away behind
a curtain, their role
in life simply to
prepare food and give
birth to children.

We were scared, but
our fear was not as
strong as our
courage.

Then they told me about
the call from home and
that they were taking
the threats seriously.
I don't know why, but
hearing I was being
targeted did not worry
me. It seemed to me that
everyone knows they
will die one day. My
feeling was nobody can
stop death; it doesn't
matter if it comes from
a Talib or cancer. So I
should do whatever I
want to do.

My father wanted us to be inspired by our great hero, but in a manner fit for our times—with pens, not swords. Just as Khattak had wanted the Pashtuns to unite against a foreign enemy, so we needed to unite against ignorance.

My mother always told me, hide your face- people are looking at you. I would reply, It does not matter; I am also looking at them.

I don't mind if I have
to sit on the floor at
school. All I want is
education. And I'm
afraid of no one.

I think everyone makes a mistake at least once in their life. The important thing is what you learn from it. That's why I have problems with our Pashtunwali code. We are supposed to take revenge for wrongs done to us, but where does that end? If a man in one family is killed or hurt by another man, revenge must be exacted to restore nang (honor).

With guns you can
kill terrorists, with
education you can
kill terrorism.

As we crossed the Malakand Pass I saw a young girl selling oranges. She was scratching marks on a piece of paper with a pencil to account for the oranges she had sold, as she could not read or write. I took a photo of her and vowed I would do everything in my power to help educate girls just like her. This was the war I was going to fight.

No struggle can ever
succeed without
women participating
side by side with men.
There are two powers
in the world; one is
the sword and the
other is the pen.
There is a third
power stronger than
both, that of women.

For my brothers it
was easy to think
about the future.
They can be anything
they want. But for me
it was hard and for
that reason I wanted
to become educated
and empower myself
with knowledge.

In some parts of the
world, students are
going to school every
day. It's their normal
life. But in other
part of the world, we
are starving for
education... it's like
a precious gift. It's
like a diamond.

In Pakistan when women
say they want
independence, people
think this means we don't
want to obey our fathers,
brothers or husbands. But
it does not mean that. It
means we want to make
decisions for ourselves.
We want to be free to go to
school or to go to work.
Nowhere is it written in
the Quran that a woman
should be dependent on a
man. The word has not
come down from the
heavens to tell us that
every woman should
listen to a man.

I told myself, Malala,
you have already
faced death. This is
your second life.
Don't be afraid — if
you are afraid, you
can't move forward.

When he [father] went
to France to collect
an award for me, he
told the audience, "In
my part of the world
most people are known
by their sons. I am
one of the few lucky
fathers known by his
daughter."

There was a time when women activists asked men to stand up for their rights. But this time we will do it by ourselves. I am not telling men to step away from speaking for women's rights, but I am focusing on women to be independent and fight for themselves.

I don't want to be
remembered as the
girl who was shot.
I want to be
remembered as the
girl who stood up.

President Barack Obama and
his family. I was respectful,
I believe, but I told him I
did not like his drone
strikes on Pakistan, that
when they kill one bad
person, innocent people are
killed, too, and terrorism
spreads more. I also told him
that if America spent less
money on weapons and war
and more on education, the
world would be a better
place. If God has given you a
voice, I decided, you must
use it even if it is to
disagree with the president
of the United States.

I think life is always
dangerous. Some
people get afraid of
it. Some people don't
go forward. But some
people, if they want
to achieve their goal,
they have to go. They
have to move.

If we want to end
terrorism we need to
bring quality
education so we
defeat the mindset of
terrorism mentality
and of hatred.

I reassured my mother that it didn't matter to me if my face was not symmetrical. Me, who had always cared about my appearance, how my hair looked! But when you see death, things change. It doesn't matter if I can't smile or blink properly, I told her. I'm still me, Malala. The important thing is God has given me my life.

We should not be
followers of traditions
that go against human
rights...we are human
beings and we make
traditions.

I started thinking about that, and I used to think that the Talib would come, and he would just kill me. But then I said, 'If he comes, what would you do Malala?' then I would reply to myself, 'Malala, just take a shoe and hit him.' But then I said, 'If you hit a Talib with your shoe, then there would be no difference between you and the Talib. You must not treat others with cruelty and that much harshly, you must fight others but through peace and through dialogue and through education.' Then I said I will tell him how important education is and that 'I even want education for your children as well.' And I will tell him, 'That's what I want to tell you, now do what you want.'

People say Malala's voice is being sold to the world. But I see it as Malala's voice reaching the world and resonating globally. You should think about what is behind Malala's voice. What is she saying? I am only talking about education, women's rights, and peace.

We are human beings,
and this is the part
of our human nature,
that we don't learn
the importance of
anything until it's
snatched from our
hands.

What a strange world
it was when a girl
who wanted to go to
school had to defy
militants with
machine guns – as
well as her own
family.

We liked to be known
as the clever girls.
When we decorated
our hands with henna
for holidays and
weddings, we drew
calculus and
chemical formulae
instead of flowers
and butterflies.

If a woman can go to
the beach and wear
nothing, then why
can't she also wear
everything?

I think it's time
that people update
themselves, educate
themselves, and
inform themselves.

Education is our right,
I said. Just as it is our
right to sing. Islam has
given us this right and
says that every girl and
boy should go to school.
The Quran says we
should seek knowledge,
study hard and learn
the mysteries of our
world.

We felt like the
Taliban saw us as
little dolls to
control, telling us
what to do and how to
dress. I thought if
God wanted us to be
like that He wouldn't
have made us all
different.

At night our fear is
strong . . . but in the
morning, in the
light, we find our
courage again.

I speak not for
myself, but so those
without a voice can be
heard. Those who have
fought for their
rights. Their right to
live in peace. Their
right to be treated
with dignity. Their
right to equality of
opportunity. Their
right to be educated.

I truly believe the
only way we can
create global peace
is through not only
educating our minds,
but our hearts and
our souls.

There is no greater
weapon than
knowledge and no
greater source of
knowledge than the
written word.

Let us make our
future now, and let us
make our dreams
tomorrow's reality.

My father was convinced the Taliban would hunt him down and kill him, but he again refused security from the police. 'If you go around with a lot of security the Taliban will use Kalashnikovs or suicide bombers and more people will be killed,' he said. 'At least I'll be killed alone.'

I love physics because
it is about truth, a
world determined by
principles and laws—
no messing around or
twisting things like
in politics...

I don't cover my face
because I want to
show my identity.

You know, my father was a great encouragement for me because he spoke out for women's rights, he spoke out for girl's education. And at that time I said that why should I wait for someone else, why should I be looking to the government, to the army that they would help us? Why don't I raise my voice, why don't we speak up for our rights?

If we believe in
something greater
than our lives, then
our voices will only
multiply even if we
are dead.

Through my story I want
to tell other children
all around the world that
they should stand up for
their rights. They should
not wait for someone else
and their voices are more
powerful. Their voices -
it would seem that they
are weak, but at the time
when no one speak, your
voice gets so loud that
everyone has to listen to
it. Everyone has to hear
it. So it's my message to
children all around the
world that they should
stand up for their
rights.

I think everyone
makes a mistake at
least once in their
life. The important
thing is what you
learn from it.

It's hard to have a gun
and kill people. Maybe
that's why his hand was
shaking. Maybe he
didn't know if he could
do it. But people are
brainwashed. That's
why they do things
like suicide attacks
and killing people. I
can't imagine it - that
boy who shot me, I can't
imagine hurting him
even with a needle.
I believe in peace.
I believe in mercy.

How great God is! He has
given us eyes to see the
beauty of the world,
hands to touch it, a nose
to experience all its
fragrance, and a heart
to appreciate it all.
But we don't realize how
miraculous our senses
are until we lose one.

In Pakistan, when we were stopped from going to school, at that time I realized that education ... Is the power for women, and that's why the terrorists are afraid of education.

I am convinced
Socialism is the only
answer and I urge all
comrades to take this
struggle to a
victorious conclusion.
Only this will free us
from the chains of
bigotry and
exploitation.

("Historic 32nd congress of
Pakistani section of IMT - First
Day". Malala Yousafzai's statement
to 32nd Congress of Pakistani
Marxists)

I had two options. One was to remain silent and wait to be killed. And the second was to speak up and then be killed. I chose the second one. I decided to speak up.